# UP YOUR GAME
## On and Off the Ice

**Rachel Stuckey**

**CRABTREE**
Publishing Company
www.crabtreebooks.com

**Author:** Rachel Stuckey

**Publishing plan research and development:**
 Reagan Miller, Crabtree Publishing Company

**Editors:** Marcia Abramson, Kelly Spence

**Proofreader:** Wendy Scavuzzo

**Photo research:** Melissa McClellan

**Cover Design:** Samara Parent

**Design:** T. J. Choleva

**Prepress technician:** Samara Parent

**Print and production coordinator:**
 Katherine Berti

**Consultant:**
Jeff Reynolds, Technical Director of hockey
for Chedoke Minor hockey

Developed and produced for Crabtree Publishing
by BlueAppleWorks Inc.

**Illustrations:** © Atula Siriwardane (p 6 bottom); Public Domain: Ysangkok (p 7)

**Photographs:**
**Front Cover: Shutterstock:** © Fotokvadrat
**Interior:** © Andy Cruz (p 15 top, 15 bottom, 19) /
**Bigstock:** © katatonia82 (p 6–7 bottom); © Paha_L (p 13 toop);
**Creative Commons:** © s.yume (p 28 bottom);
**iStockphoto:** © LSOphoto (title page, p 21 top left); © vanhoffen (p 6 right);
**Keystone Press:** © Colorado Springs Gazette (p 23 bottom right);
© Chris Szagola (p 27);
**Public Domain:** Ysangkok (p 7); Chicago Blackhawks/NHL (p 24 left);
**Shutterstock.com:** © Scott Prokop (TOC); © B Calkins (page toppers);
© Iurii Osadchi (p 4, 6–7 top, 17 bottom, 24–25 top); © Shooter Bob Square
Lenses (hand & puck); © Uralskiy Ivan (p 5 top); © Roberto Zilli (p 5 bottom);
© Pavel L Photo and Video (p 10, 20); © iofoto (p 11, 14, 17 top); © Christopher
Penler (p. 12–13 top); © Pukhov Konstantin (p. 12–13 bottom); © Pixart
(P 12 left); © muzsy (p 13 bottom); © katatonia82 (p 16 left); © Herbert Kratky
(p 16 right); © Jai Agnish (p 18–19); © Debby Wong (p 18 left); © Alhovik (p 20);
© Lorraine Swanson (p 21 top right); © photosthatrock (p 21 bottom left);
© Michael Chamberlin (p 22); © Lilyana Vynogradova (p 23 middle); © Pukhov
Konstantin (p 24–25 bottom); © Laszlo Szirtesi (p 24 right); © BrunoRosa
(p 25 top); © Vladislav Gajic (p 26); © Samo Trebizan (p 29 top); verca
(p 29 right top); © Lilyana Vynogradova (p 29 right bottom); © Lorraine
Swanson (p 30) /
© Stephen Wise (p 6 left, 8, 9, 23 top)

**Library and Archives Canada Cataloguing in Publication**

Stuckey, Rachel, author
        Up your game on and off the ice / Rachel Stuckey.

(Hockey source)
Includes index.
Issued in print and electronic formats.
ISBN 978-0-7787-0772-1 (bound).--ISBN 978-0-7787-0723-3 (pbk.).--
ISBN 978-1-4271-7683-7 (pdf).--ISBN 978-1-4271-7679-0 (html)

        1. Hockey--Training--Juvenile literature.  I. Title.

GV848.3.S78 2014          j796.96207          C2014-903834-8
                                              C2014-903835-6

**Library of Congress Cataloging-in-Publication Data**

CIP available at the Library of Congress

# Crabtree Publishing Company

Printed in the U.S.A./092014/JA20140811

www.crabtreebooks.com      1-800-387-7650

**Published in Canada**
**Crabtree Publishing**
616 Welland Ave.
St. Catharines, ON
L2M 5V6

**Published in the United States**
**Crabtree Publishing**
PMB 59051
350 Fifth Avenue, 59th Floor
New York, New York 10118

**Published in the United Kingdom**
**Crabtree Publishing**
Maritime House
Basin Road North, Hove
BN41 1WR

**Published in Australia**
**Crabtree Publishing**
3 Charles Street
Coburg North
VIC 3058

# TABLE OF CONTENTS

HOCKEY
Source

## LET'S PLAY HOCKEY!

# HOCKEY AROUND THE WORLD

Hockey is one of the fastest and most exciting games on Earth. The sport is most popular in Canada, the Czech Republic, Finland, Russia, Slovakia, Sweden, and the United States. There are many different hockey **leagues** for both men and women at **professional**, **amateur**, and **recreational** levels.

## Hockey Leagues in North America

The NHL (National Hockey League) is the major men's professional hockey league in North America. There are also minor professional hockey teams. The Canadian Women's Hockey League (CWHL) is a professional women's league with five teams—four in Canada and one in the United States.

*Hockey is a popular Olympic sport. At the 2014 Olympics in Sochi, Russia, the American and Canadian women's hockey teams played for the gold medal. Team Canada won the close game in overtime.*

## Around the World

Some countries have men's and women's national teams. They compete in world championships and the Olympics. The International Ice Hockey Federation (IIHF) organizes international competition for players of all ages. Many NHL players also play for their **native**, or home, country's team during these exciting international events.

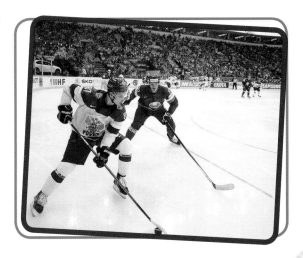

*International hockey competitions are popular events that showcase some of the world's best hockey players.*

### Cool Fact!

There are different kinds of hockey played around the world—and many not on ice. Field hockey is played on grass or turf. Roller hockey is played on in-line skates, with a ball. Speed, skill, and strategy are important skills to practice, no matter what kind of hockey you play.

## Sledge Hockey

**Sledge** hockey is played by individuals with **disabilities**. Players sit on a sledge, or sled, and play with shorter sticks. The sticks are used to shoot, pass, and move around the ice. Sledge hockey is one of the most popular sports in the **Paralympics**, a special competition for athletes with physical disabilites.

*In the United States, sledge hockey is known as sled hockey.*

5

# HOW TO PLAY

Hockey is played by two **opposing** teams. There are three forwards, two defenders, and one goalie from each team on the ice. Each team tries to score goals by shooting the puck into the other team's net.

*Hockey players wear skates, shin pads, padded pants, shoulder and elbow pads, gloves, and helmets. Goalies also wear special pads, gloves, and helmets with facemasks.*

*Hockey is a team sport and it takes a lot of energy to play! Groups of players play together in **lines**, or shifts. The forward lines change often to give these players a rest during the game. Defense lines change as well, but not as often. The goalie usually plays the whole game.*

## The Rink

A hockey rink is divided into different **zones**, or sections, by red and blue lines. A thick red **center line** divides the rink in half. Two thinner red lines in each end mark the **goal line**. Two **blue lines** between the center line and goal line create the **neutral zone**. Fives circles on the ice are for **face-offs**. There are also two **penalty boxes** on one side of the rink. Boards surround the rink to keep the puck—and players—from flying into the crowd!

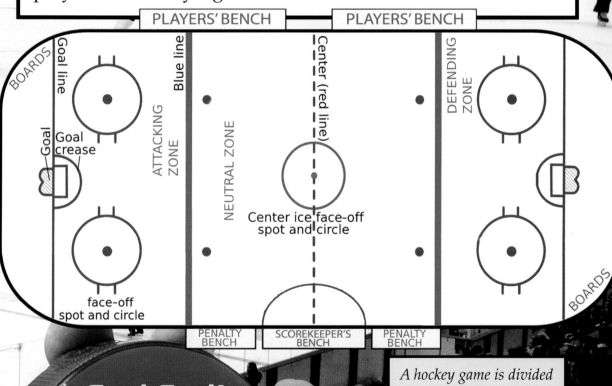

PLAYERS' BENCH    PLAYERS' BENCH

BOARDS

Goal line

Blue line

ATTACKING ZONE

NEUTRAL ZONE

Center (red line)

DEFENDING ZONE

Goal

Goal crease

Center ice face-off spot and circle

face-off spot and circle

BOARDS

PENALTY BENCH    SCOREKEEPER'S BENCH    PENALTY BENCH

## Cool Fact!

In North America, a hockey rink is 85 feet (26 m) wide and 200 feet (61 m) long. In Europe and international competitions, the rink is 98 feet (30 m) wide.

*A hockey game is divided into three 20-minute periods. The teams switch ends each period. The end your team is protecting is called the **defending** zone. The end you are trying to score in is called the **attacking zone**.*

# WARMING UP

Hockey is a physically demanding sport. It is important to warm up before you begin playing. Playing sports when your muscles are cold can cause injury. It's also important to get your heart pumping and warm up your muscles before you stretch. Making sure your muscles are loose and warm will keep you strong and injury free.

## Don't Stand Still!

You can warm up on or off the ice. On the ice, you can skate laps to loosen your muscles. Off the ice, warm up your body with **dynamic**, or active, stretches and exercises.

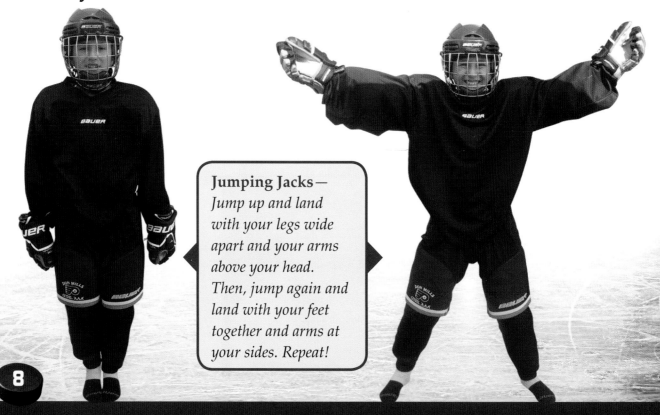

**Jumping Jacks—** *Jump up and land with your legs wide apart and your arms above your head. Then, jump again and land with your feet together and arms at your sides. Repeat!*

8

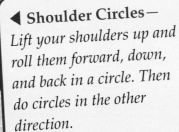

**Arm Swings**—*Stand with your feet apart and bend a little at the knee. Keep your arms straight and move them in circles from front to back and back to front. Bend a little at the waist and knees to move with the circles.*

◀ **Shoulder Circles**—*Lift your shoulders up and roll them forward, down, and back in a circle. Then do circles in the other direction.*

## Other Get-Moving Warmups

**Heel Kickers**—Run across the room, lifting your heels as high as they go. Pump your arms as you lift your knees.

**Leg Swings**—Hold on to a chair or the wall and stand tall on one leg. Swing the other leg from front to back.

**Lunges**—Step forward with one leg and bend at the knee. Then lift your back leg up to walk forward and bend at the knee again.

**Running High Knees**—Walk across a room, lifting your knees as high as they go. Try to take as many steps as you can. Pump your arms as you lift your knees.

# SKATING SKILLS

Skating is the most important skill for any hockey player. Hockey players must have excellent balance and **agility** to move quickly and easily in any direction and at high speeds. To skate like a hockey player, start in the correct position: leaning forward with your back straight. Your feet should be shoulder-width apart and your knees should be bent.

## Glide and Drive

Skating in hockey is a little different than skating just for fun. Keep your knees bent with the blades of both skates flat on the ice. Use one leg to drive or push against the ice and glide across the ice on the other. Shift your weight from your drive leg to your glide leg and repeat. The trick is to try not to take your skates off the ice when driving, gliding, and shifting your weight. It might take a bit of practice, but don't give up!

*Stay low while you skate. Power and speed come from your legs.*

## Moving Around

After you learn to glide and drive, you must learn how to put on the brakes with a hockey stop. Using the inside edge of your skate, gently push out against the ice. Don't push down—just shave off the top layer of the ice. Be sure to practice stopping on both sides. Start slow. As you improve, practice your hockey stop while skating faster.

## Crossovers

**Crossovers** are a skating technique that help you move quickly on the ice. To practice, start skating slowly in a circle with your knees bent. To crossover to the left, lift your right skate and bring it in front of your left skate. Use the inside edge of your left skate to push against the ice. Then bring your left leg back to the left and forward. Practice crossing over in both directions. Remember to stay low and lean into the circle.

### The Stop and Go Drill

This easy drill will have you stopping like a pro in no time!
Begin at one side of the rink on the goal line.
Skate hard to the first blue line and stop.
Skate back to the goal line and stop.
Skate to the center line and stop.
Skate back to the blue line and stop.
Skate to the other blue line and stop.
Skate back to the center line and stop.
Skate all the way to the opposite goal line.
Repeat in the other direction.

# PUCK CONTROL

A hockey puck is a hard disk of **vulcanized** rubber. A standard puck is black and 1 inch (25 mm) thick. The length from one edge to the other is 3 inches (76 mm). Usually, every player on the ice will touch the puck during a game. Learning how to control the puck is key to your success on or off the ice!

## Stick Handling

Before you can control the puck, you must learn to handle your stick. Hold your stick correctly and keep your wrists flexible. The first step to handling the puck is to practice your puck control. Stand still on the ice and practice moving the puck from side to side in different ways.

*You can practice your stick and puck handling skills on your own.*

## Moving Puck Control

The next step is to practice your puck control while moving. The best test of your puck control and stick handling is to do it while practicing your skating. You can also practice on or off the ice using a golf ball instead of a puck to focus on speed and control.

*Skating with a puck between pylons can help improve your puck-handling control.*

## Passing Skills

The best hockey players are team players! To pass the puck, put your weight on your back skate and sweep the puck across the ice in front of you. Follow through to your target. The most important part of receiving a pass is to keep the puck from bouncing off your stick. Angle your blade slightly toward the ice to create a pocket to receive the puck in.

### The Passing Drill

Practice your control by skating up and down the rink with a partner and passing the puck back and forth.

### Cool Fact!

The fastest player in the NHL is Carl Hagelin. In 2012, he won the NHL All-Star Fastest Skater competition with a time of 12.993 seconds. Hagelin holds the record for best final time in the competition's 20-year history.

*Practice your passing with your teammates to master the skill.*

# SHOOTING AND SCORING

Any player on the ice can score a goal. Most are scored by forwards, but defensemen also score goals. At the end of the season, the NHL player who has scored the most goals wins the Art Ross Trophy. Wayne Gretzky won the trophy 10 times in 20 years. Bobby Orr is the only defenseman to win the trophy, and he won it twice!

## Wrist Shot

There are different ways to shoot a hockey puck. The **wrist shot** is the first shot players should learn because it is the most **accurate**. Begin with the puck at your back skate and trap it with your stick by rolling your wrists forward. Roll your wrists back as you sweep the puck toward your front skate. Roll your wrists forward again to release the puck.

### The Shooting Drill

Skate the length of the rink with the puck. Every three feet, shoot the puck against the boards to practice your wrist shot.

*A wrist shot is far more accurate than a **slap shot**.*

## Slap Shot

The slap shot is the most powerful shot in hockey, but it is not always accurate. Start with the puck in front of you and pull your stick back, but not too high. Roll your wrists forward as you swing your stick forward. As you hit the puck, roll your wrists back to release the puck with a snap! It's important to shift your weight and use your body to add power to the shot.

*Practice your slap shot to make it accurate.*

## Tips and Deflections

Things happen fast in a hockey game, and you don't always have the time and space to set up the perfect shot. Many goals are scored with **tips** and **deflections**. Tips are shots that use your blade or stick to redirect the puck toward the net. Deflections are shots that change direction when they hit a player, blade, or stick. If you are in front of the net, you can tip or deflect the puck in to score!

*Tip and deflection shots are extremely hard for goalies to defend against.*

### Cool Fact!

In the NHL, the average speed of a wrist shot is about 55 miles per hour (88.5 kph). The average NHL slap shot is about 87 miles per hour (140 kph). Zdeno Chára has the fastest slap shot in the NHL. His shot is over 100 miles per hour (161 kph)!

# CHECKING

Players use checking to stop other players from passing and shooting. There are many types of checking. The two most common types are **stick checking** and **body checking**.

*Angling can be considered the first line of defense for hockey players.*

## Positioning and Angling

The first step to check another player is positioning and **angling**. By positioning yourself between the player with the puck and his or her teammates, you can stop a pass. Angling forces your opponents to go in the direction you want them to go in.

*Stick checking may be considered the second line of defense.*

## Stick Checking

You can use your stick to control your opponent's stick. In a **poke check**, you use your stick to knock the puck away from another player. In a **sweep check**, you use your stick to pull or push the puck away or to keep the other player from passing.

## Body Checking

Body checking is the last step in defense. In a body check, a player uses the force of his or her body to knock their opponent away from the puck. You can only check another player who has the puck. Most countries have banned body checking in youth hockey. This protects younger players from injuries and allows them to focus on developing their skills. Passing, stick handling, shooting, and skating are key skills to master.

*Body checking is the third step in hockey defense **tactics**, or strategies.*

## Faster, Cleaner Hockey

There is no checking allowed in women's hockey at any level. Some fans believe this is not fair and that women are just as tough as men. But others believe women's hockey is faster and more exciting because there is no body checking. No body checking also means there is less fighting in women's hockey!

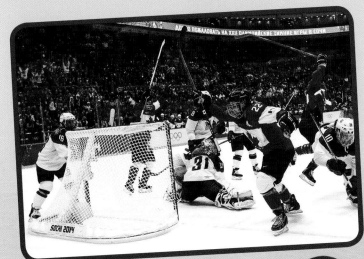

*Women's hockey is different than men's because body checking is not allowed. This makes games faster and cleaner.*

# FACING OFF

A face-off is how play begins in hockey. A player from each team lines up at the face-off circle. The referee drops the puck onto the dot in the circle and each player tries to win control of the puck. Usually, it's the centers that participate in face-offs, but sometimes the left and right wingers take them. If you play center, your stick will probably break more often than your teammates'. Adding extra tape to your stick will help protect it from breaking if it hits your opponent's stick.

## Face-Off Circles

There are five face-off circles on a hockey rink and four extra face-off spots. One circle is the center of the ice, and there is one circle in each corner of the rink. The four face-off dots are in the neutral zone. At the beginning of each period, there is a face-off at center ice. During the period, the referee uses the face-off circle closest to where the play ended to begin play again.

### Cool Fact!

Jonathan Toews is one of the best face-off players in the NHL. In 2013, Toews won 834 face-offs. On average, he wins three out of every five face-offs!

*Jonathan Toews (far left) shows off his skills with a ball at an NHL celebration.*

## Job for Center Forwards

As a center, one of your jobs on the ice is to win face-offs. There are many face-off strategies and it's important to practice them with your teammates. Wingers and defensemen all have important jobs during a face-off. Each player must either help win the puck or keep the other team from doing so. Centers should practice face-offs as much as they can, but your team should also practice face-off plays so you all know what to do when you win the puck!

## How to Win a Face-Off

Keep your knees bent and stay close to the ice.
**Choke up**, or move your hands down, on your stick.
Grip your stick tightly.
Line up your skates, hips, and shoulders square to the circle.
Have a plan or strategy with your team.
Practice, practice, practice!

*Hockey players at every level need to practice face-offs. Winning face-offs is key to winning games. In a typical NHL game, referees call about 60 face-offs!*

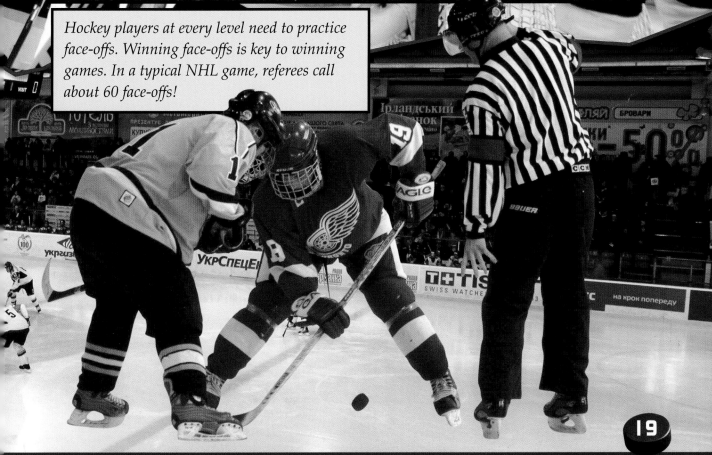

# FORWARDS

Forwards score most of the goals in hockey. The center, right wing, and left wing work together to get past the other team's defense. Forwards have to watch that they do not go **offside**. Attacking players cannot cross the other team's blue line with their skates before the puck does, or they are called offside. Forwards have to be careful when they have control of the puck. They cannot pass the puck down the ice to a teammate near the goal. Forwards must also come back to help their defensemen in the defensive zone. They go after **rebounds**, or loose pucks, cover open players, and block the **shooting lanes**.

## Where to Shoot?

Goalies must cover five basic areas, often called **scoring zones**. There is one zone for each of the goalie's arms and legs. The fifth is between the goalie's legs, and it is called the **five hole**. The numbering usually goes like this:

1. Stick-side low
2. Glove-side low
3. Glove-side high
4. Stick-side high
5. Between the legs

*It takes a long time to become a goal-scoring superstar. Practicing the stop and start drill is a great way to get you there!*

*You don't need ice time to work on your shooting skills. You can practice off-ice with a ball.*

## Stop and Start Drill

The stop and start drill is a good way to practice your forward skills. Start at the face-off circle next to the net. Skate toward the neutral zone with the puck and stop, then start skating again. After stopping and starting one more time, make a **power turn** toward the goal and take a shot.

## Sidney Crosby

Sidney Crosby is one of the best forwards in the game. His speed helps him avoid defenders. This gives him lots of good chances to score goals. Crosby started playing for the Pittsburgh Penguins when he was just 18 years old. He scored the gold-winning goal for Canada at the 2010 Winter Olympics in Vancouver.

# DEFENSEMEN

The job of the defensemen is to keep the other team from scoring goals by stopping them from passing and shooting the puck at the net. Defensemen also try to force the other team's forwards into the corners of the defensive zone. When their team is on offense, defensemen usually play on the blue line so they can stop the puck if it comes back toward their net.

*Defensemen must be excellent skaters. Skating backward is an important skill for defensemen to master.*

# You Shoot, You Score!

Defensemen also score goals. Some defensive players are known as "offensive defensive" players and help score lots of goals. Other defenders concentrate on defensive play. When defensemen score goals, it's usually from far away. They have to work hard on their slap shots.

*It is also important for defensemen to have great wrist shots!*

## Puck in the Middle Drill

Three players pass the puck to each other with one defender in the middle. When the defender intercepts a pass, he or she trades places with the passer.

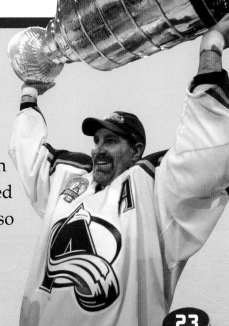

## Ray Bourque

Ray Bourque played 22 seasons in the NHL. He was a Boston Bruin for 21 years. Bourque holds records for most career goals, assists, and points by a defenseman. He was also team captain longer than any other NHL player. Bourque played his final year with the Colorado Avalanche. He also played for the Canadian Olympic hockey team.

*Ray Bourque only won the Stanley Cup once—in his final game in the last season he played!*

# GOALTENDER

The goaltender, or goalie, stands in front of the net and stops the puck. Stopping a shot on goal is called a **save**. If a goalie stops all the shots in a game and the other team never scores, it is called a **shutout**. Hockey is a mental game for goalies— they must always be focused on the next shot. They must stay positive and confident, even if the other team scores. Goalies don't get to take breaks like other players. They usually stay in net for the whole game.

## Butterfly Goalie

In the **butterfly** style of goaltending, the goalie drops to his or her knees to block shots. When they are on their knees, goalies look like butterflies! This style is different from the older **stand-up** style, where goalies use their feet to stop the puck. Butterfly style became more popular when goalies started wearing facemasks. With their faces protected, goalies get their bodies closer to the ice, forcing shooters to aim for the top half of the net.

*Tony Esposito was one of the pioneers of the now popular butterfly style. He is a retired Canadian-American NHL goaltender, remembered in the Hockey Hall of Fame.*

## Combining Styles

The **hybrid** style of goaltending is a combination of the older stand-up style and the butterfly style. Most goalies today use a hybrid style. It is more difficult to guess what a goalie is going to do if he or she uses both the butterfly and stand-up styles. Hybrid goalies are very flexible!

## Playing the Angles

The best goalies play the **angles**. They know how to position themselves to stop a shot before the player shoots. Hockey pucks move fast, so goalies cannot wait to react. Sometimes a goalie will leave the crease to cut down the angle or the amount of net an offensive player can see. But this is risky because it can leave the net open for another player to score.

## Cool Fact!

In 1994, Dominik Hašek made 70 saves in a single game shutout. Known as "the Dominator", Hašek still holds the record for the highest number of saves in an NHL shutout game.

## Catch and Drop Drill

Goaltenders should practice the catch and drop on and off the ice. Have a friend throw pucks or tennis balls at you quickly. Catch them in your goalie glove and drop them to the ice or ground. It's best to have at least 10 pucks or balls.

# REFEREES AND THE RULES

In pro hockey, two referees and two linesmen **officiate**, or direct, each game. They all wear striped jerseys, but have different jobs. Other levels of hockey have fewer on-ice officials.

## Referees

Referees, who wear orange or red armbands, supervise the game and make sure that play is fair. This includes giving out **penalties** for breaking rules. Referees whistle to signal when a goal has been scored and when play has been stopped.

## Linesmen

The linesmen watch for line violations, such as when players are offside, and stop play when they occur. They handle all face-offs except at the start of a period and after a goal, when a referee drops the puck. Linesmen often help referees make the final call on a play. It is also their job to stop fights!

*Two referees and two linesmen are on the ice to make the calls in most professional hockey games.*

## Penalty!

**Minor**, **major**, and **match** penalties are called when a player breaks a rule. When a minor penalty is called, a player is sent to the penalty box for two minutes. This gives the other team a **power play**. For major penalties, a player is sent to the box for five minutes. This gives one team lots of time to score while the other is **short-handed**, or down players. Match penalties are when a player is removed from a game and can lead to game suspensions. Match penalties give the other team a power play, and another player on the penalized team must serve time in the penalty box.

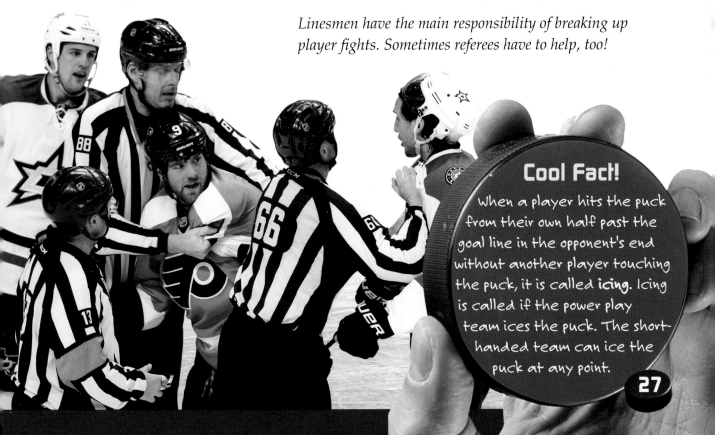

*Linesmen have the main responsibility of breaking up player fights. Sometimes referees have to help, too!*

### Cool Fact!

When a player hits the puck from their own half past the goal line in the opponent's end without another player touching the puck, it is called **icing**. Icing is called if the power play team ices the puck. The short-handed team can ice the puck at any point.

# THE ALL-AROUND PLAYER

Hockey is an energetic and physical game. But, sometimes, the excitement of competition can lead to conflict. Good sportsmanship is very important in any sport, including hockey. Winning may be important, but the best players focus more on their passion for the sport than on winning the game. You must play fair, follow the rules, respect the judgment of referees, and respect the other team. Whether you win or lose, congratulate your opponents and teammates on a game well played.

## See Yourself Succeed

Play happens fast in hockey. It's important to stay positive and focus on playing well. This is called the mental game. **Visualize** or imagine yourself doing well and, when you hit the ice, you will!

*Good sportsmanship means celebrating victories without being disrespectful to your opponents or teammates.*

## Off-Ice Training

Hockey takes a lot of energy. Strength and **endurance** are very important. When you are not playing hockey, you can **crosstrain** for the sport by running and in-line skating. Other kinds of exercise are good, too—including strength training, swimming, other sports, and stretching. Some players even take dance lessons to practice balance and footwork.

*In-line skates were developed as a substitute for ice skates. In-line skating helps improve your fitness and balance, while also working out the muscles used for ice hockey.*

## The Importance of Nutrition

Eating properly will help you play better. Athletes need to eat extra calories because they burn up lots of energy. But you also need the right calories. It's important to choose foods with lots of nutrients and good quality carbohydrates and proteins. Stay away from junk! You must also stay hydrated. Young hockey players lose about 2 quarts (1.89 L) of water a day! It's important to replace that water before, during, and after playing.

*To avoid dehydration, you can drink water and sports beverages.*

# LEARN LIKE THE PROS

The best hockey players work very hard. on the **fundamentals**, or basic skills, of the game. Working on your skills on your own will make your team practices better and your game play even better. Ask your coaches and teammates for feedback on how you can continue to become the best player you can be. You can also improve your skills by taking power skating lessons, playing in summer leagues, and going to hockey camp!

## For the Love of the Game

At any age level, you can play competitive or non-competitive hockey. Good sportsmanship, nutrition, teamwork, and practice all make hockey a great sport at all levels. No matter whether you play for fun or competitively, remember to have fun!

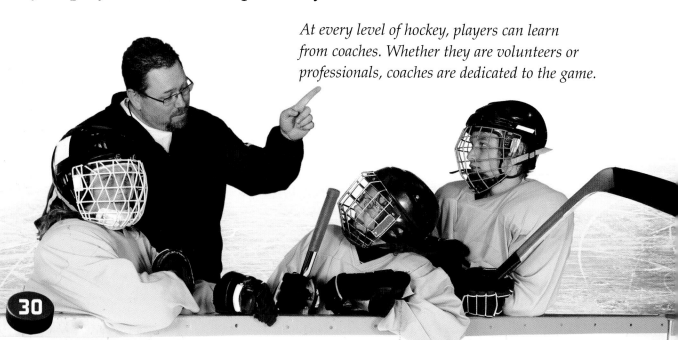

*At every level of hockey, players can learn from coaches. Whether they are volunteers or professionals, coaches are dedicated to the game.*

# LEARNING MORE

Check out these books and websites to find out more about the fastest game on Earth.

## Books

*Play Better Hockey: 50 Essential Skills for Player Development* by Ron Davidson, Firefly Books, 2010

*Hockey Skills: How to Play Like a Pro* by James MacDonald, Enslow Publishers, 2008

## Websites

Hockey USA: Players and Parents
The official site of USA Hockey.
www.usahockey.com/page/show/753607-players-and-parents

Hockey Canada: Programs
The official site of Hockey Canada.
www.hockeycanada.ca/en-ca/hockey-programs.aspx

NHL Learn to Play
Learn from the pros at this NHL site for kids. There are tips for offense, defense, and goalies.
www.nhl.com/kids/subpage/learn.html

# GLOSSARY

**Please note: Some boldfaced words are defined where they appear in the book.**

**accurate** Free from mistakes

**agility** The ability to move quickly and easily

**amateur** When someone plays for fun without getting paid

**angling** Moving or directing

**crosstrain** To train in other sports to improve your skills or level of fitness

**disabilities** Mental or physical restrictions that affect the performance of tasks

**endurance** The ability to do something for a long time

**face-offs** In hockey, how play starts after a penalty or goal

**hybrid** Something that is formed by combining two or more things

**leagues** Organized groups of teams that compete against one another

**opposing** On the other side, either in location or with respect to team play

**penalties** Punishments for breaking a rule in sports

**penalty boxes** The areas off to one side of a hockey rink where players must serve a penalty

**power play** When one team has more players on the ice than the other team

**power turn** A tight turn players make while skating fast

**professional** A person who is paid to play a sport

**recreational** Playing for fun

**shooting lanes** Lines from the puck to the net

**shutout** A game in which one team never scores a goal

**slap shot** A hard type of shot

**visualize** To make a picture of something in your mind

**vulcanized** Hardened by using heat and sulfur or a similar process

# INDEX